W9-AGD-273

551.48
Sil

314

Our World
RIVERS AND LAKES

Theodore Rowland-Entwistle

Silver Burdett Press
Morristown, New Jersey

Titles in this series

Mountains

Rivers and Lakes

Deserts

Jungles and Rainforests

Polar Regions

Seas and Oceans

First published in 1986 by
Wayland (Publishers) Ltd
61 Western Road, Hove
East Sussex BN3 1JD

Adapted and first published
in the United States in 1987 by
Silver Burdett Press,
250 James Street,
Morristown, New Jersey 07960

© Copyright 1986 Wayland (Publishers) Ltd

© 1987 This adaptation
Silver Burdett Press.

All Rights Reserved.

Designed by Malcolm Smythe

U.S. Edition edited by Joanne Fink

Front cover, main picture San Raphael Fall, Ecuador.
Front cover, inset The common frog of Britain,
Europe, and Asia.
Back cover Kachura Lake, Pakistan.

Library of Congress Cataloging-in-Publication Data

Rowland-Entwistle, Theodore.
  Rivers and lakes.

  (Our world)
  Includes bibliographies and index.
  Summary: Describes the characteristics of different kinds of
rivers and lakes and their importance to the surrounding plant,
animal and human life.
    1. Rivers – Juvenile literature. 2. Lakes – Juvenile literature.
[1. Rivers. 2. Lakes]
I. Title.   II. Series.
GB 1203.8.R68   1987   551.48'3   87-12679
ISBN 0-382-09499-9

Typeset by Alphabet Limited, London
Printed in Italy by G. Canale & C.S.p.A., Turin

Contents

Kinds of rivers

All rivers have small beginnings. The most usual source of a river is a spring, from which water bubbles up out of the ground. Some rivers flow out of lakes, which are themselves fed by springs. Streams in mountainous areas are fed by the melting of winter snows or of glaciers – rivers of slowly-moving ice.

Rivers rise on high ground, flowing down on either side of ridges to sea level. The point at which the direction of flow changes is called the watershed. A large river has many smaller streams, called tributaries, flowing into it. The whole complex is a river system, and the area which is drained by this system is the river basin.

Rivers vary in type according to the terrain through which they flow. In mountainous regions, such as Norway, the rivers are fast-flowing torrents. In flat lands the rivers flow more slowly. The majority of rivers end their course in the sea, but some, such as the Volga which ends in the Caspian Sea, flow into landlocked lakes.

The section of a river where it enters the sea is called its estuary, and the water there is a mixture of fresh and salt water. The length of an estuary depends on the flatness of the ground at the river mouth and the rise and fall of the tide at that point. If the land is very flat the river may split into a number of smaller channels on its way to the sea, forming a delta – named because its shape is like that of the Greek letter $\triangle$ (delta).

In some areas, such as the central part of Australia, rain occurs for only a short time each year, and in some years may not fall at all. In such areas the rivers flow only after the rains. The rest of the time the riverbeds are dry. Such dry riverbeds are known as arroyos in the Americas, wadis in the Sahara and southwestern Asia, and nullahs in the Indian subcontinent. By contrast, in cold regions where snow and ice lie all year round, a mass of ice may move slowly down a valley to form a glacier.

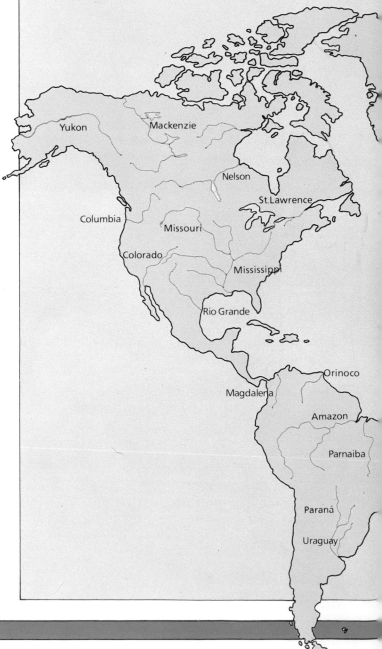

Major rivers of the world
The largest river system in the world, when measured both by the size of the area it drains and by the volume of water it discharges into the sea, is the Amazon. The Nile is the longest river in the world with a length of 4,145 miles (6,670 km) but the Amazon is almost as long at 4,000 miles

(6,437 km). The third longest river is the Mississippi-Missouri system (3,860 miles or 6,210 km) which is also the longest on the North American continent. The Chang Jiang (Yangtze) of China is the longest river in Asia and the fourth longest in the world. The second longest river in Africa is the Zaire which is the tenth longest in the world but the second largest in terms of basin size and the volume of water it discharges. The longest river in Europe is the Russian river the Volga (2,290 miles or 3,690 km) but it is only the sixteenth longest in the world. The shortest river in the world is the D River in Oregon, which is a mere 440 ft (134 m) long. It connects a lake with the ocean.

Classifying rivers

There are several ways of describing the different reaches or sections of rivers, based on the kind of landscape through which the river runs. The upper reach of a river is fast-flowing, as it makes its way through mountainous country. The water is cold, and few plants can get a root-hold in it because of the speed of the current. Often there are no fish in this part of the river. The middle reach lies in the lowlands. The stream flows more gently, and a great many different kinds of plants can live in the shallow water along its banks.

The lower reach of a river is similar to the middle reach, but the rate of flow is slower still. The river wanders over a wide flood plain, a flat area which is quickly flooded when the river is in spate – that is, full of water from heavy rains or melting snow.

In Western Europe the parts of a river are sometimes classified according to the kinds of fish that live in them, such as the troutbeck, with trout living in it, the minnow or grayling reach, and the bream reach, which contains bream and similar species of fish.

A river may follow a natural fold in the ground,

Rapids

Rapids are parts of the river where the water flows faster than usual and is very turbulent. Rapids occur where the river suddenly steepens for a distance or where a river narrows. They are often caused by a layer of harder rock that lies in the same direction as the river and outcrops in the river bed. Rapids are common in mountains.

Soft rock   Hard rock   Soft rock

or wear a course through the rock. A river channel cut through rock can be very deep indeed. The finest example is the Grand Canyon of the Colorado River. Over several million years the Colorado has carved a great gash in the earth, more than 1 mile (1.6 km) deep and varying in width from 14 to 18 miles (23 to 29 km).

Flowing water always takes the line of least resistance, so a river cuts its way through soft rock and leaves harder rock. This is why rivers follow winding courses. A waterfall is often produced when a river comes to a bed of hard rock lying on top of softer rocks. The soft rock is gradually worn away, leaving a sill of the hard rock, over which the water cascades. From time to time the edge of the sill breaks away, so the waterfall is constantly receding upstream. Rapids are like a series of miniature waterfalls. They are often formed by a layer of hard rock between layers of softer rock. The hard rock layer points upstream and projects into the river bed. The slope of the river flattens before the hard rock and steepens as it flows over it.

Left The Blue Nile Falls, Bahar Dar, Ethiopia.

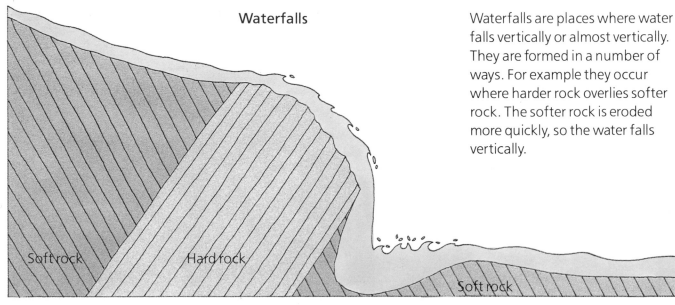

Waterfalls

Waterfalls are places where water falls vertically or almost vertically. They are formed in a number of ways. For example they occur where harder rock overlies softer rock. The softer rock is eroded more quickly, so the water falls vertically.

Softrock

Hard rock

Soft rock

The water cycle

One of the most important functions of rivers is the part they play in the hydrological or water cycle – the system by which water is distributed over the earth's surface. Every year the heat of the sun evaporates the equivalent of a layer of water 3.3ft (1m) deep all over the surface of the world's oceans. This water falls back to the earth's surface as rain. Nine-tenths of it falls on the sea. The remaining tenth falls on the land, and in due course finds its way back into the sea. Most of it is carried there by rivers but some, called ground water, flows to the sea underground.

This is a slight simplification, because some water is also evaporated from rivers and lakes, while plants transpire (release) large quantities of water through their leaves. But even when all this is taken into account, the world's rivers carry enormous quantities of water down to the oceans every year.

Rivers flowing through tropical rain forests, such as the Zaire River of Africa, hold a fairly constant amount of water, but in regions where there is a definite rainy season, such as the monsoon in Asia, the rivers are low in the dry season and may flood disastrously after the rains.

River water, although it is fresh in contrast to the salt of the sea, contains various chemicals. It also differs in chemical content from rainwater.

The water or hydrological cycle is the result of two natural forces – the heat of the sun and gravity. The heat of the sun evaporates water from the sea. This water in the form of vapor rises into the atmosphere and cools into tiny droplets or ice crystals, that form clouds. The clouds may be carried inland by the wind and as they pass over the land they may collect more water vapor, which is

Clouds

Precipitation – rain, hail, or snow

Evaporation from lakes

Water returned to the sea by rivers and as ground water

Rivers can be very destructive especially when they flood. This bridge in Iran is being destroyed by a flooded river. This shows some of the enormous energy involved in the water cycle.

Rain is slightly acidic, because it picks up a certain amount of carbon dioxide from the atmosphere. Where the air is heavily polluted by industry we get the "acid rain" that is thought to be causing so much damage to North American and European trees.

As rainwater seeps through the ground it dissolves some of the minerals in rocks and soil, so when it reaches a river as ground water it carries some of those minerals with it. The chemical content of the river may vary along its course. If it rises in an area of heavy clay, it is likely to be very acidic, but if it then flows through limestone or chalk it becomes more alkaline.

released by plants in a process called transpiration. We do not know precisely what causes clouds to release their water — in the form of rain, hail, or snow — but when a cloud has to rise to cross hills or mountains it often releases water. Gravity draws the water downward. It collects in streams that flow into rivers and down to the sea. Water also flows underground to the sea.

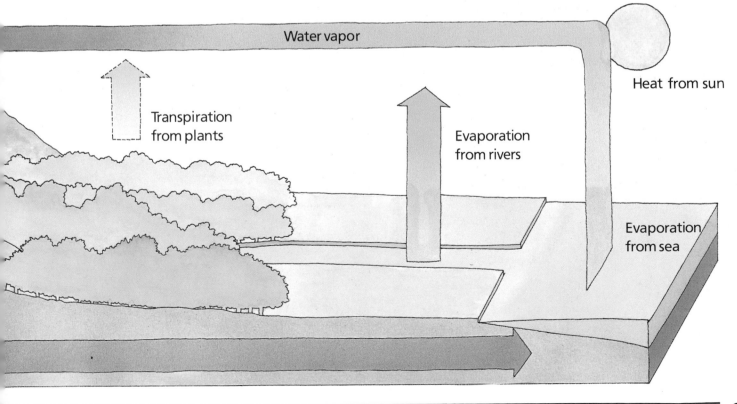

Water vapor

Heat from sun

Transpiration from plants

Evaporation from rivers

Evaporation from sea

Wearing away the land

Rivers play a major part in the process of erosion, which is constantly wearing away the surface of the land. The action of water on rocks is almost as powerful as if a giant scraper were in action. Rock is broken up as water in it freezes and expands, or as its minerals dissolve away. Rain and wind also help to wear away rock. The resulting debris is carried away by rivers.

In its early, swift-flowing stage a river can carry along gravel, stones, and even large boulders. As it slows down it deposits the larger rocks, but it continues to carry sediment (particles of soil) until it reaches the sea, where it deposits them. Layers of such sediments, deposited over millions of years, are eventually converted into sedimentary rocks. The amount of sediment carried by rivers is enormous. For example, the Rhône River in France carries 530,000,000 cubic feet (15,000,000 cubic meters) of soil into the Mediterranean Sea every year.

Besides carrying soil and other material that has washed into them, rivers also actively erode the land. A strong current can dislodge and lift particles from the river bed, and the friction produced by rocks bounding along the stream wears away other rocks. A river flowing through a limestone region may actually disappear, because it finds its way into the cracks that are a feature of this rock, and so flows underground.

1 Youthful river
The youthful part of a river begins at the source. The amount of water it carries is small but it is fast flowing. At first it runs over the landscape but farther down it begins to cut into it, forming a V-shaped valley.

2 Mature river
The mature river flows in a deep V-shaped valley but the river soon begins to cut into the sides of the valley and it also deposits soil to form a flat valley bottom. Small bends or meanders form as it winds over the valley floor.

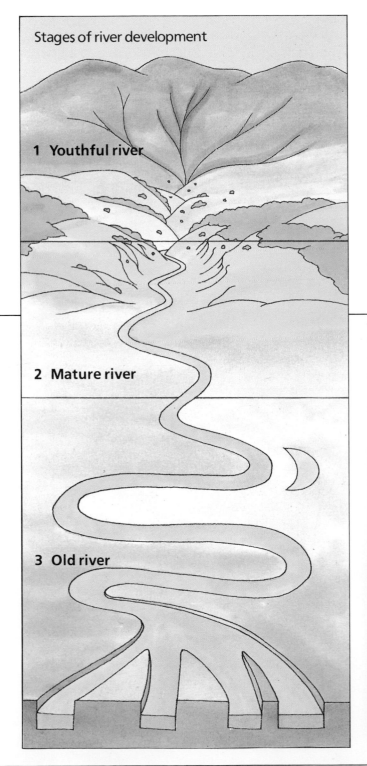

Stages of river development

1 Youthful river

2 Mature river

3 Old river

As it encounters soft ground the river cuts a concave curve, with a steep bank. On the other side it deposits some of the material it is carrying. Eventually the meander may form an almost complete circle. The force of the current then cuts across the remaining section of the circle and a short straight stretch of river results. The abandoned meander is gradually cut off by an accumulation of silt to form a lake, known as an ox-bow lake or bayou.

Flooding rivers deposit silt on either side, which builds up to form high banks called levees. A slow-flowing river also deposits silt in its bed, so in time the river may actually be flowing in a channel above the level of the flood plain.

3 Old river

In old age the river flows across a broad flood plain, as the flat land that is covered by water when the river floods is called. It develops large meanders — the river bends back on itself in great loops. It finishes at the sea.

Life in the upper reaches

A stream that rises in the low hills of a lowland region may have much the same plant and animal life for most of its length. But an upland stream, rising amid rocky mountains, has a character all its own. The water flows swiftly along a steep, rocky bed, interspersed with waterfalls and rapids. Such streams have little sediment where plants can find a roothold. But there are nooks in even the fastest streams, where mosses, liverworts, and algae can flourish.

Only those animals that can resist a fast-flowing current can live in upland streams.

They include the nymphs (young stages of insects that develop in water) of mayflies and stoneflies, and the larvae of caddisflies. In the northern hemisphere the main fish found in such streams is the trout, which likes fast-running water.

As the current becomes gentler more species of plants flourish, such as water crowfoot, reeds, and pondweeds, and there are many kinds of fish feeding on the abundant insect nymphs, eggs, and larvae. Water beetles are common, and so are shelled animals such as water snails. In areas where there is very little calcium in the water,

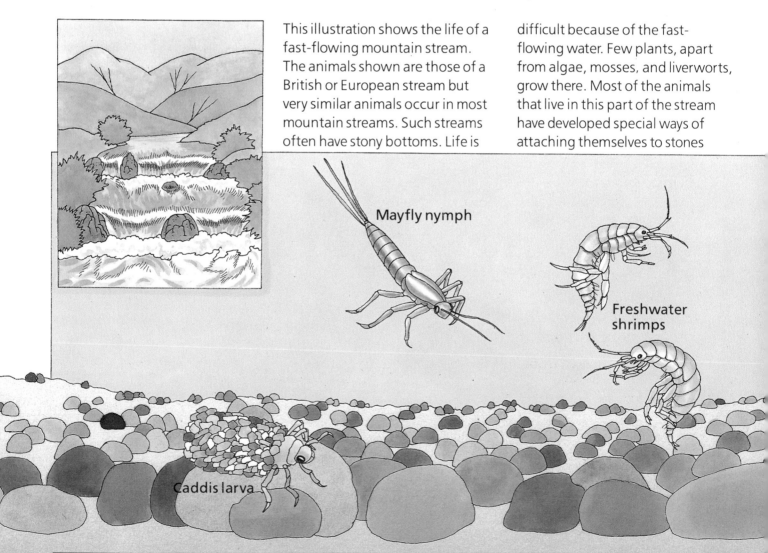

This illustration shows the life of a fast-flowing mountain stream. The animals shown are those of a British or European stream but very similar animals occur in most mountain streams. Such streams often have stony bottoms. Life is difficult because of the fast-flowing water. Few plants, apart from algae, mosses, and liverworts, grow there. Most of the animals that live in this part of the stream have developed special ways of attaching themselves to stones

Mayfly nymph

Freshwater shrimps

Caddis larva

Some salmon migrate from the sea up rivers to high mountain streams where they breed.

snails and other shelled animals cannot flourish, because they cannot extract enough calcium to make their shells.

Local climatic conditions have a profound effect on river life. In areas that have severe winters, ice sometimes forms in the rivers and can scrape off rock plants such as mosses and algae, while heavy floods – which often follow the melting of snow and ice – can sweep away many plants. Winter floods are less damaging than summer ones, because in winter the plants are small and offer little resistance to the water.

or are flattened to escape being swept away. This environment does have its advantages. The tumbling of the water makes it full of oxygen and the temperature, although cold, is constant. Invertebrates (animals without backbones, for example, insects) such as the nymphs of mayflies and stoneflies, caddis larvae, limpets, and snails are characteristic of mountain streams, though some fish such as trout can survive here.

The brown trout of Europe is typical of this group of fish. It has been introduced into many other parts of the world. Trout have very streamlined bodies and are popular with anglers for their "fight."

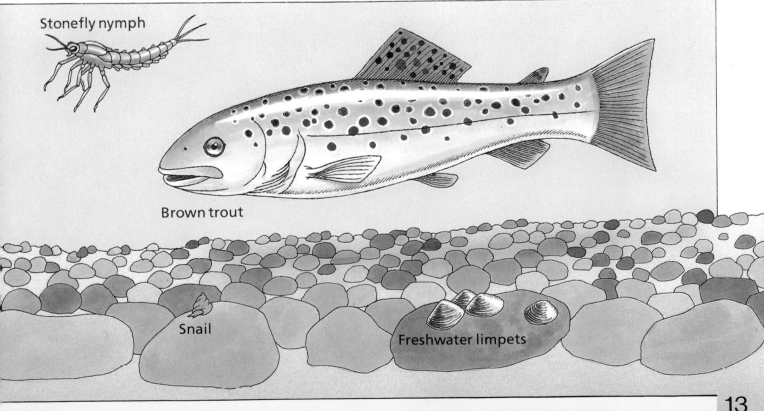

Stonefly nymph

Brown trout

Snail

Freshwater limpets

Life in the lower reaches

The rich silt that is found on the bottom of slow-flowing rivers is home for a great variety of plants, some of which grow entirely under the water except for their flowers. Near the banks rushes and similar plants grow freely. The fish in a slow-flowing river are many and various. They include bass, carp, chub, dace, perch, and pike. The fish feed on insects in various stages of development, and also on the many crustaceans that live in running water, such as copepods, freshwater shrimps, and crayfish. Other animal life includes snails and mussels, and worms that burrow in the mud.

Most of the freshwater animals cannot live in river estuaries, where sea water mingles with the fresh water. The change in saltiness is often quite sudden, and may occur as far as 25 miles (40km) inland. There are fewer animals in this stretch of the river, but they include some ocean fish and other sea creatures that can tolerate brackish (semi-salt) water, and some animals that live only in brackish water. They include species of snails, shrimps, copepods, and worms.

Most freshwater fish are harmless, but the piranhas of the Amazon River in South America are bloodthirsty. These small fish travel in groups of several thousand, and can devour a large animal in a few minutes.

The rivers of Europe and North America form the breeding grounds for an ocean fish,

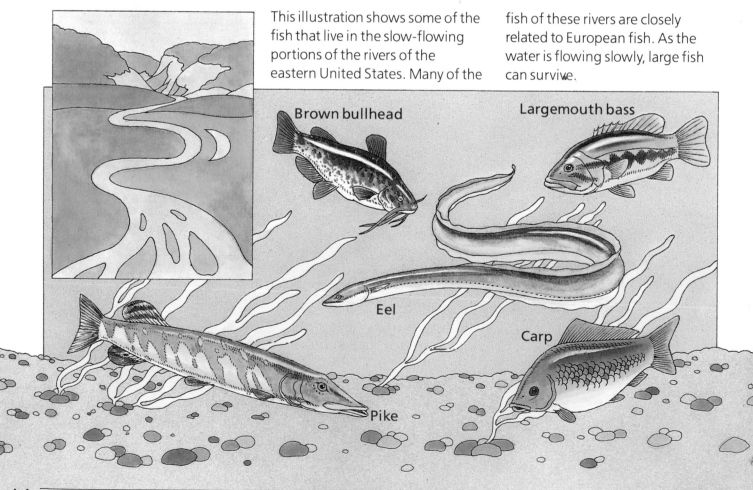

This illustration shows some of the fish that live in the slow-flowing portions of the rivers of the eastern United States. Many of the fish of these rivers are closely related to European fish. As the water is flowing slowly, large fish can survive.

Brown bullhead

Largemouth bass

Eel

Carp

Pike

Amphibians such as this frog can be found in most streams and rivers but are more common in the slow-flowing waters of the lower reaches.

the salmon. Young salmon hatch in clear mountain streams, and go to sea when they are anywhere from one to eight years old. They travel thousands of miles in the Pacific or Atlantic oceans, but eventually return to the river where they hatched out. There they breed, and most of them die. In contrast, eels of the northern hemisphere breed in the Sargasso Sea, a weed-covered stretch of the northwestern Atlantic. They cross the ocean, either to North America or Europe, and make their way upstream, where males may stay for as long as twelve years, and females for twice that time. They return to the Sargasso to breed and die. A related species of eel lives in the rivers of Australia, and breeds in the Indian Ocean.

This illustration shows some of the fish of the Nile. For much of its length the Nile is a broad, slow-flowing river that is rich in silt and therefore in life. It can support large fish, such as the Nile perch, the tiger fish, catfishes, and a species of lungfish.

The Nile also has a snail that is a host to the Bilharzia parasite which enters the blood of people who use the water and makes them sick.

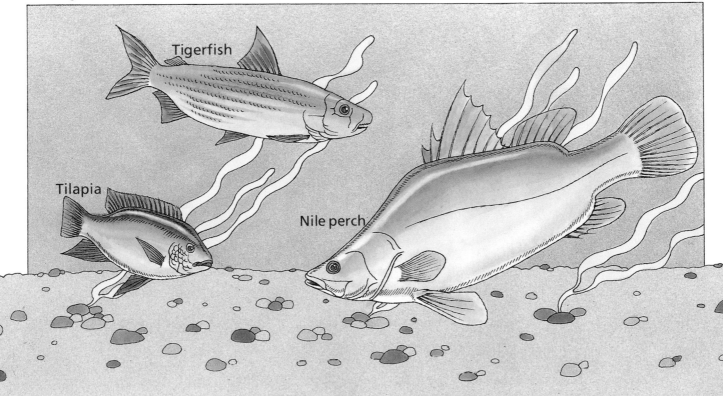

Tigerfish

Tilapia

Nile perch

Larger river animals

Many birds and mammals make their homes on or near rivers. Ducks, geese, and swans are the most familiar of the birds that swim on the water, while kingfishers make their nests in holes in river banks and catch fish for their food. Gulls and waders of all kinds are common along river estuaries, generally searching for their food in the soft mud at low tide.

Among the bank-dwelling animals is the European water vole (the Water Rat of *The Wind in the Willows*). Much larger is the graceful otter, which swims to catch its regular diet of fish, frogs and crustaceans and is known for its playfulness. Smaller but similar in build is the mink, but it is not as aquatic in its habits as the otter. In Australia the duck-billed platypus, one of only two kinds of mammals that lay eggs, has a life style very similar to that of the otter.

Other river animals include the coypu or nutria of South America, one of the largest rodents, which has been introduced into North America and Europe with disastrous results. One of the largest water animals in the northern hemisphere is the beaver, found in both North America and Europe.

In Africa, Asia, Australia, and the Americas many rivers have crocodiles or alligators among their animal life. These fierce reptiles can kill and eat very large animals, even people. Another group of reptiles found in warmer lands consists of the freshwater tortoises or turtles.

The world's largest water animal is the hippopotamus, which is found only in Africa. This huge animal spends most of the day submerged in rivers and lakes, coming on land at night to feed. On land it is clumsy, but under water it can tiptoe gracefully along on the bottom.

The hippopotamus
Hippopotamuses live in herds in the rivers, swamps, and lakes of Africa. Despite their ungainly appearance they can run as fast as a person and for short distances even faster.

The Nile crocodile
Crocodiles live in and along rivers, lakes, and marshes in the tropics and subtropics. They feed on fish, turtles, birds, and mammals. The Nile crocodile has also been known to attack people.

Rivers and river banks are usually rich in life as water is plentiful for plant growth. The flowing water carries sediments and nutrients to enrich the soil, and light is available as the river breaks the tree canopy. Where plants are plentiful so are animals. This illustration shows animals typical of the temperate parts of the northern hemisphere.

The platypus
The streams and rivers of eastern Australia are the home of the platypus. Its sensitive bill is used for finding food.

Settlement and rivers

People need water if they are to survive, so it is not surprising that the earliest civilizations were founded on the banks of rivers. The four major cradles of civilization were the Egyptian, on the Nile; the Sumerian (later Babylonian) between the Tigris and Euphrates in what is now Iraq; the Indus Valley civilization in what is now Pakistan; and the Chinese, on the Hwang-ho (Yellow River).

The most important role of these rivers was in agriculture, for it was the ability to grow crops and so settle in one place that enabled people to develop less primitive ways of life than their ancestors. In Egypt the Nile flowed through desert, but its waters provided a corridor of green and fertile land. Every year the river flooded, spreading rich silt over the farm land. The Hwang-ho also flooded, sometimes disastrously. From all these rivers people irrigated their land by digging canals and ditches to channel water over the fields.

If you look at a map you will see that most of the world's major cities still lie on the banks of rivers.

Rivers were once used for defense. At this castle in Poland the river forms a natural moat on one side, and a ditch was dug to divert the river water to create a moat on the other side.

For many people in India the Ganges River is a goddess and its water is sacred. People from all over India make pilgrimages to bathe in the river. Many millions of people also make their homes along its banks.

Irrigation

Irrigation involves the construction of artificial channels to divert the water from a river and distribute it over the fields. To do so it is often necessary to lift the water from the level of the river to that of the surrounding land. One means of doing this is the Archimedean screw, above. It consists of a spiral inside a watertight tube. The handle is turned, rotating the spiral which raises the water. Another way of raising the water level is by constructing underwater barriers that raise the level of a whole section of the river. Sometimes these are used to divert floodwater onto the fields (called basin irrigation) and sometimes to maintain a steady flow of water into canals (called perennial irrigation).

For example, London grew up on the Thames, which provided water, transportation, and defense from the south. In the turbulent times of the Middle Ages, defense was an important consideration for people planning a new town. Towns were built on islands in rivers and on river promontories, and rivers were used to create moats.

Durham, in the north of England, was built on rocky ground in a loop of the Wear River, leaving only a narrow neck of land to defend. The first settlement in Paris was on an island in the middle of the Seine, the Île de Paris.

In more modern times, colonists in America founded their settlements on river banks. And when the young United States decided to establish a new capital, President George Washington, selected a site on the banks of the Potomac River for the city that is named after him.

Because they are difficult to cross, rivers often form boundaries between parishes, counties, states, and even countries.

The Thames barrier was built to save London from flooding.

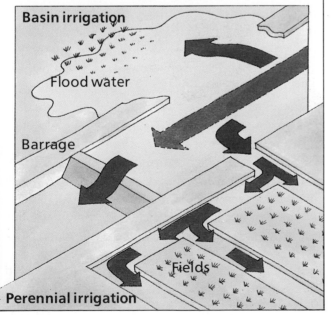

Basin irrigation

Flood water

Barrage

Fields

Perennial irrigation

Rivers for transportation

Rivers can hinder as well as help transportation. Here a ferry has to be used to transport motor vehicles across a river that cuts across a road.

This is a steamboat on the Mississippi, near New Orleans. These boats were used for carrying freight and passengers but are now used to carry tourists.

For thousands of years, rivers were the main means of travel and communication. Even today they are important in many parts of the world, especially North America and continental Europe. Heavy loads can be carried easily on the wide rivers of these two regions, and canals have been constructed to link the rivers.

The most important rivers of Europe are the Rhine, in the west; the Danube, which rises in the Black Forest area of Germany and flows eastward to the Black Sea; and the Dnieper, Don, and Volga in the Soviet Union. In the United States the outstanding river network is provided by the Mississippi and its main tributaries, the Missouri, Illinois, Ohio, and Arkansas rivers.

Many rivers, such as the Nile and the Zaire River, are navigable for only part of their length, because of natural barriers such as waterfalls and rapids. When people seek to travel on such rivers they have to resort to portages – that is, carrying boats over land around obstacles such as rapids. But, only small boats can be carried in this way.

In recent years a great deal has been done to make rivers more useful for transportation. For example, the Russians have dredged the Dnieper to deepen it so that boats can travel along most of its entire length. Where rapids are in the way the river has been dammed, and locks have been installed so that boats can go up and down from one level of the river to another.

Rivers need constant care to keep them in suitable condition for traffic. They must be dredged, to remove accumulations of silt, and their banks must be protected. A river tends to wear away its banks, and many rivers, such as the Thames in London, now flow between stone walls or embankments that prevent such erosion.

Right A barge on the Rhine. These barges are used for transporting such freight as coal, petroleum products, and building materials.

Power from rivers

The flow of water downhill provides a valuable source of energy, and one that cannot be used up like coal, oil, or nuclear fuels. The first use of rivers to provide power was to drive waterwheels. The earliest water wheels were used for milling corn, and the buildings in which this work was done were known as watermills. When the Industrial Revolution began in the 1700s, the first factories were established along river banks where there was a source of power.

There are two kinds of waterwheels. The earliest had blades that dipped into the water, and turned the wheel as the stream flowed along underneath it. This undershot wheel was not very efficient. Later the overshot wheel was developed. It has scooplike buckets around it, and water flows into these buckets over the top of the wheel. The weight of the water in the buckets helps the force of the stream to turn the wheel. The overshot wheel is about 80% efficient, but to use it a fall of water is necessary. This is usually achieved by damming the river to create a millpond, from which the water flows. Another advantage of the millpond is that it delivers the water to the wheel at a constant rate.

Today, hydroelectric systems use the power of rivers to produce electricity. They are most often found in places where the rivers flow steeply downhill and so produce ample power. Huge dams are built, creating giant reservoirs, and the waterwheels used, called turbines, mostly lie horizontally. Norway, where the rivers flow very steeply indeed, is able to produce almost all its electricity from hydroelectric systems.

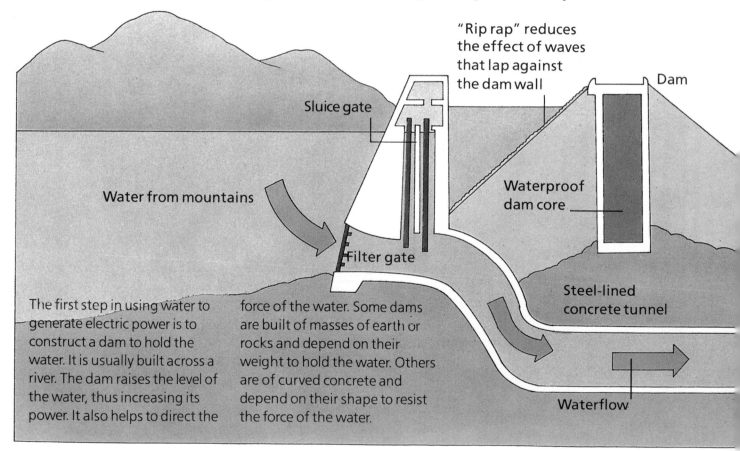

"Rip rap" reduces the effect of waves that lap against the dam wall

Dam

Sluice gate

Waterproof dam core

Water from mountains

Filter gate

Steel-lined concrete tunnel

Waterflow

The first step in using water to generate electric power is to construct a dam to hold the water. It is usually built across a river. The dam raises the level of the water, thus increasing its power. It also helps to direct the force of the water. Some dams are built of masses of earth or rocks and depend on their weight to hold the water. Others are of curved concrete and depend on their shape to resist the force of the water.

The water rushing into the spillway of the Itaipu Dam in Brazil suggests the enormous power of water. After passing through the turbine, the water still has tremendous force. Spillways are constructed to control and channel this force, which otherwise could erode away the base of the dam. Spillways are also used to divert floodwaters, which could destroy the dam.

The Itaipu Dam is the largest producer of hydroelectricity in the world.

Water is a cheap, renewable form of energy. The initial cost of building a dam and power station is high but the source of energy is free.

Countries with high mountains that have a plentiful rainfall, for example Norway, are ideal for hydroelectric generation. With the development of multi-use dams, for example for irrigation as well, hydroelectric power has become practicable elsewhere. Major dams are being built in many countries.

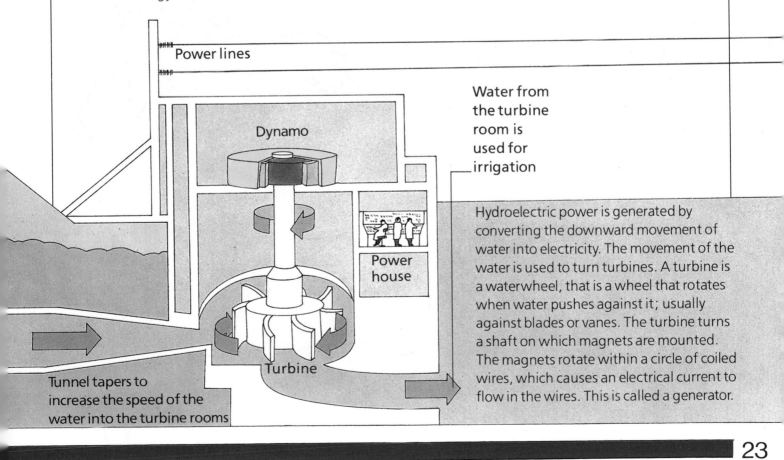

Power lines

Dynamo

Water from the turbine room is used for irrigation

Power house

Turbine

Tunnel tapers to increase the speed of the water into the turbine rooms

Hydroelectric power is generated by converting the downward movement of water into electricity. The movement of the water is used to turn turbines. A turbine is a waterwheel, that is a wheel that rotates when water pushes against it; usually against blades or vanes. The turbine turns a shaft on which magnets are mounted. The magnets rotate within a circle of coiled wires, which causes an electrical current to flow in the wires. This is called a generator.

Kinds of lakes

Lakes vary greatly in character depending on where they are and how they are fed, rather than on how they were formed. Most lakes contain fresh water, but a number are salty. Salt lakes have no outlet, so the minerals that wash into them from the surrounding rocks are trapped. They are found in very hot, dry areas. One of the most salty of all is the Dead Sea, which is nine times as salty as the oceans. Although large quantities of fresh water pour into it from the Jordan River and other streams, most of this water evaporates in the intense heat of the region. Few plants grow there and no fish live in it.

Other examples include the Great Salt Lake in Utah, and Lake Eyre, which is Australia's largest lake when there is any water in it. For most of the time the surface of Lake Eyre is covered by a salt crust that can be as much as 15ft (4.5m) thick. It fills only in times of exceptional rainfall. In the early 1980s it was full for two successive years.

The freshwater lake with the largest surface area in the world is Lake Superior, one of the five Great Lakes of North America. The second largest is Lake Victoria, in Africa, the main source of the Nile River. The largest freshwater lake by volume is Lake Baikal in Siberia.

Many lakes are shrinking or disappearing in our own time. Lake Chad in north-central Africa varies in size from season to season, but overall it is gradually getting smaller. The Caspian Sea is also shrinking, largely as a result of human activity: water from the rivers that feed it is being diverted for irrigation. One lake that vanished and then reappeared is Lop Nor, in central Asia. The river that fed it shifted its course in about A.D. 330, and the lake disappeared, while another lake, the Kara-Koshun, came into existence. Lop Nor reappeared in 1921 when the course of the river was diverted. Further interference with the river caused Lop Nor to dry up once again in 1964.

Freshwater lake
Lake Superior on the Canadian-U.S. border.

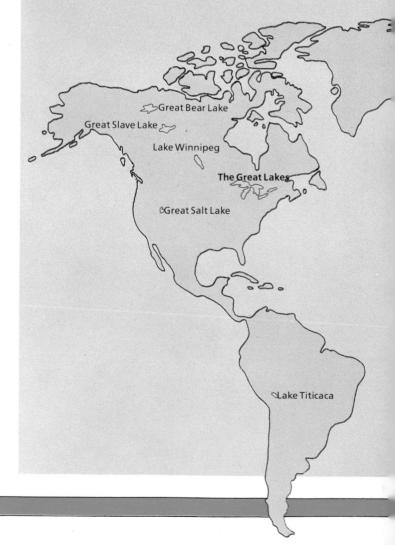

Great Bear Lake

Great Slave Lake

Lake Winnipeg

The Great Lakes

Great Salt Lake

Lake Titicaca

Salt lake
The Great Salt Lake in Utah.

Dry or seasonal lake
Lake Torrens, Australia.

Lake Baikal

Aral Sea

Caspian Sea

Dead Sea

Lop Nor

Lake Chad

Lake Rudolph

Lake Victoria

Lake Tanganyika

Lake Malawi

Lake Eyre

Lake Torrens

Major lakes of the world

The largest lake in the world by both surface area and volume is the Caspian Sea. It is also the largest salt lake. The freshwater lake with the largest surface area is Lake Superior, which is part of the Great Lakes system of North America. This system is the world's greatest array of large lakes. The freshwater lake with the most water is Lake Baikal in southwestern Siberia. It is also the deepest lake in the world although it is only the third largest by surface area in the Soviet Union and eighth largest in the world. The highest, navigable lake is Lake Titicaca on the Peru-Bolivia border, while the lowest lake is the Dead Sea, a salt lake, which lies on the border of Israel and Jordan.

How lakes are formed

Lakes form in various ways in hollows in the land. In geological terms they are short-lived because the rivers that fill them with water also tend to fill them with silt, and the rivers that empty them tend to wear away the rim and let the water out.

Many lakes of northern Europe, Asia, and North America were formed during the last ice age, when the ice cap covered these regions. Glaciers carved deep hollows and valleys in mountain rocks. The glaciers also dammed the valleys by carrying down large quantities of rock and other debris and piling them up in what is known as a moraine. Most of Britain's lakes were formed in this way. Some countries, such as Canada, have enormous numbers of glacial lakes; Finland, a much smaller country, has as many as 60,000.

Faults and movements of the earth's crust have produced lakes, notable examples being the world's lowest lake, the Dead Sea, which lies between Jordan and Israel and is about 1,300ft (400m) below sea level, measured from its surface; the largest lake, the Caspian Sea, which lies between Europe and Asia; and the deepest lake, Lake Baikal in southern Siberia, which is 5,700ft (1,740m) deep.

Lakes are sometimes formed when water accumulates in the craters of extinct volcanoes. Crater Lake in Oregon is an outstanding example.

In limestone regions water hollows out huge caverns where rivers flow, or used to flow. Some of these caverns contain underground lakes. In others, the roof has collapsed, leaving a hollow where a surface lake can form.

Landslides can produce lakes by damming rivers. Such lakes are usually very short-lived because the dam is made of loose, unstable material. A lagoon is created when the sea throws up a bank of pebbles or sand close to the shore, trapping water behind it. The waters of lagoons are generally salty or brackish.

Crater Lake in Oregon. As its name suggests it is a lake that has formed in the crater of a volcano.

Glacial lakes

The most common way lakes are formed is by glacial action. Glaciers are rivers of ice formed when there is a massive build-up of snow in cold regions. The weight of the snow above turns the lower layers of snow to ice and this ice begins to flow slowly downhill. In the past, when the climate was colder, glaciers formed great sheets called ice caps. Where there were ice caps in the past there are now many lakes, for example, in northern Canada. In high mountains glaciers also form. These glaciers sometimes retreat leaving lakes behind them. Glaciers create lakes in two ways, either by cutting into the land to make a hollow or by depositing pieces of rock, which form a barrier that water collects behind.

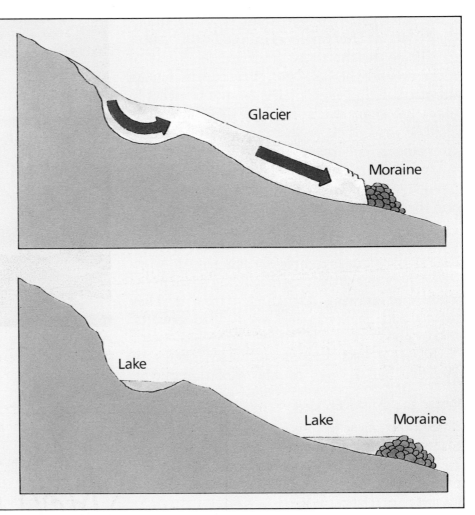

Lakes often form in limestone regions. Limestone is dissolved by rainwater that contains carbon-dioxide. The water seeps underground and into cracks in the rock. This water may collect in a large underground river, which can hollow out huge caverns. In some of these caverns lakes form. If these caverns are near the surface they may collapse and a lake may sometimes form in the hollow that is created.

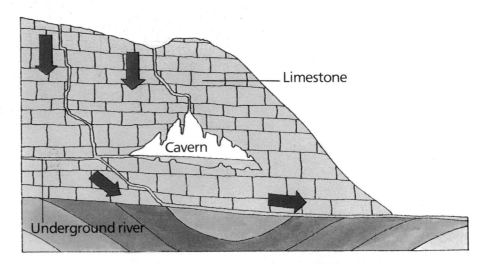

Plant life in lakes

Lakes vary greatly in the kinds of living things they contain. This variety is caused by differences in climate, height above sea level, the kinds of rocks around the lake and, increasingly, human interference. In general, lakes tend to be richer in plant life than rivers, because they have more shallow areas, their water is not flowing, and the rivers that supply them bring in quantities of rich silt, which forms a good bed for vegetation. Plants provide food and homes for many water animals, and they also supply oxygen to the water.

Most lake plants grow near the edges of lakes because their roots need to be anchored in mud, even if the plant is completely submerged. A few plants float freely, their roots hanging down in the water and drawing nourishment from it. They include such plants as duckweeds, bladderworts, and frogbit.

Unless a lake has steep, rocky shores, it probably has a wide, marshy region around it,

Although the flower of the water hyacinth is beautiful, the plant is a pest, threatening to clog many lakes and rivers in the warmer parts of the world.

The plant life of lakes can be divided into four zones. The plants shown here grow in many parts of the world. The swamp plant zone has plants that are rooted in very shallow water, which sometimes dries leaving the plants exposed. The typical plants of this zone are rushes and sedges. The floating-leaf and emergent zone has plants that are truly aquatic, since the water doesn't dry up. The leaves and flowers either float on the surface or poke up into the air. In the submerged plant zone the plants live under water. The free-floating plant zone has plants such as duckweed that float on the surface.

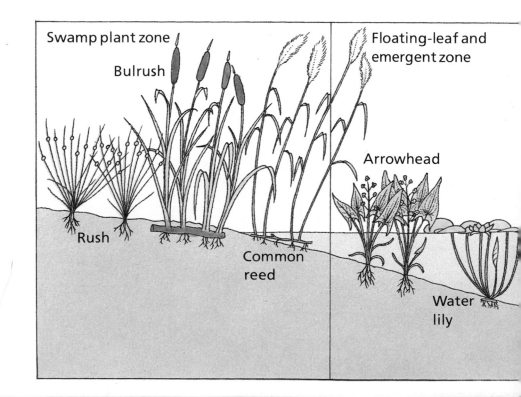

Swamp plant zone
Bulrush
Rush
Common reed
Floating-leaf and emergent zone
Arrowhead
Water lily

which merges into the permanent waters of the lake. The plants of this region include rushes and sedges, willowherbs, marsh marigolds, and bur reeds. A number of trees such as alder and willow, which like a damp situation, often grow near lakes. Farther out from the shore are such plants as waterlilies and pondweeds. Nearly all the flowering plants have their flowers above water, even if the rest of the plant is submerged. Exceptions include the hornworts, which bloom underwater.

There are a number of non-flowering plants. Around the edge there are mosses. The still waters of lakes may be covered with millions of tiny plants, many too small to see except through a microscope. They are water fungi, sometimes called watermolds, and algae. There are also many bacteria, simple organisms that are not strictly plants or animals, and other microscopic organisms such as amoebas.

This is the great water lily, originally from the Amazon basin. Its leaves range from 4 ft (1.22m) to 6 ft (1.8m) in diameter.

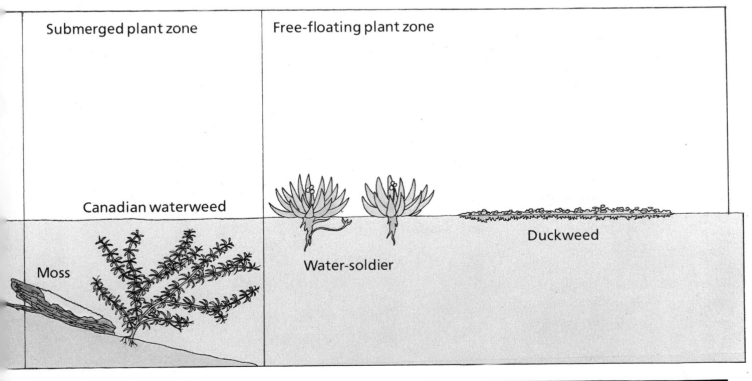

Submerged plant zone

Free-floating plant zone

Canadian waterweed

Water-soldier

Duckweed

Moss

Animal life in lakes

The animal life of lakes varies as greatly as the plant life, and for the same reasons. Generally speaking, it resembles that of the slower-flowing reaches of a river. However, since lakes are basically bodies of still water, the kind of animal life is affected by additional factors.

One factor is temperature, and this usually varies with the seasons. In winter the water is a uniform temperature from top to bottom, generally around 39°F (4°C). In warm weather, the upper layer of water in a lake heats up rapidly, while the bottom of the lake remains cold. The warm upper layer is known as the epilimnion, and the cold lower layer as the hypolimnion. Between the two layers is a zone called the thermocline.

Various insect larvae, crustaceans, and worms live in the mud at the bottom of lakes. They depend for at least part of their nourishment on a steady rain of decaying plant and animal life that

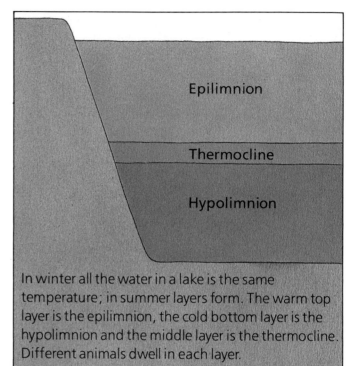

In winter all the water in a lake is the same temperature; in summer layers form. The warm top layer is the epilimnion, the cold bottom layer is the hypolimnion and the middle layer is the thermocline. Different animals dwell in each layer.

Many different types of birds can live on one lake because they can reach food at different depths. This illustration shows how the birds of a lake in southeastern Australia can use different parts of the lake. The Cape Barren goose grazes on the shore. The coot also feeds on the shore, although it can also swim and bob for food. The pink-eared duck searches along the water's edge for food. The chestnut teal upends and feeds on the lake bottom, as do the mallard and the black swan but at greater depths. The greatest depths are reached by diving birds such as the white-eyed duck, while the southern shoveler feeds on the surface.

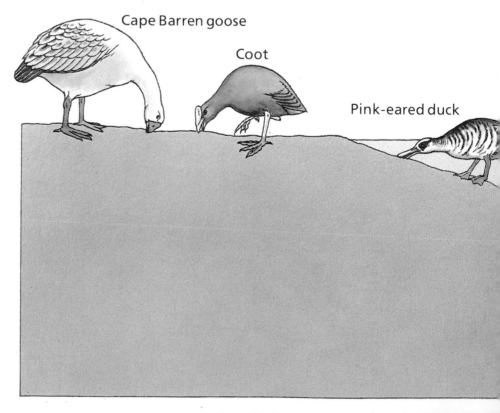

Tortoises or freshwater turtles are common inhabitants of many lakes, especially in the warmer parts of the world. In temperate climates they often hibernate during winter in the mud at the bottom of the lakes or ponds.

falls from above. Their existence is limited by the amount of oxygen available. As organic matter decays, oxygen is absorbed, and during the summer months supplies of fresh oxygen to the bottom layer of a lake may be very small indeed. If the oxygen becomes completely depleted the only organisms that can thrive are certain bacteria, known as anaerobic bacteria because they can live without oxygen. The kinds of fish found depend on oxygen levels. Trout and minnows require ample supplies of oxygen, while carp, tench, and bream can survive with low amounts of oxygen.

The numbers of animals present in a lake depend also on whether it is oligotrophic – that is, poorly supplied with nutrients – or eutrophic – rich in nutrients. Eutrophic lakes often have dense layers of algae, appearing generally as a green scum. They are generally richer in plant and animal life.

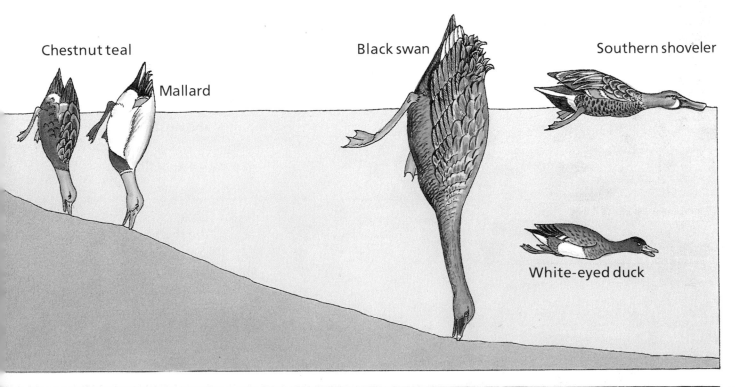

Chestnut teal

Mallard

Black swan

Southern shoveler

White-eyed duck

Living by lakes

People have been living beside lakes for thousands of years. As with rivers, lakes provided a supply of water, easy transportation in canoes, and defense against attack on one side at least.

From living beside a lake it was only a step to living over the lake, so that water provided protection on all sides. Remains of prehistoric houses built on stilts in former lake beds have been found in many countries. Notable examples are to be found in England and in the Alpine lakes of Switzerland, Germany, Italy, and France. Others have been discovered in eastern Europe. Many of these dwellings seem to have been built in the marshes around lakes rather than in the lakes themselves, and examples of this kind of dwelling are found today in parts of Southeast Asia, such as Malaysia. On Pacific islands, similar dwellings are built on the edge of lagoons.

One striking lake village is rebuilt twice a year.

It is in the Tonle Sap, a large lake in Cambodia that is rich in fish. In the dry season the people of the region drive piles into the muddy bottom of the lake and erect their huts on platforms on top of the piles. During the wet monsoon season the lake floods, and the pile village is then moved back onto dry land.

One of the biggest lake settlements of today is in the marshlands of southern Iraq, where the Tigris and Euphrates rivers meet. The Ma'dan, the marsh Arabs, make their homes here on artificial islands. Each island is made by building a fence of reeds around a patch of swamp, and heaping into the enclosure mud and reeds woven into mats. The Ma'dan use reeds to make their long, tunnel-like houses. The reeds are also sold for roofing throughout Iraq and the reed shoots are food for the water buffalo. The Ma'dan travel around their watery homeland by canoe, catching fish.

Left People have lived beside lakes in Europe for many hundreds of years. This is the town of Hallstatt, on a lake in Upper Austria, which has been occupied for 1,600 years. The town has given its name to a period of the early Iron Age of central and western Europe, since many remains of this period have been discovered there.

Right The Aymara Indians live around the shores of Lake Titicaca. One of the earliest civilizations of the Americas developed here. The Aymara grow crops such as potatoes and corn on terraced fields around the shore and catch fish in the lake.

Using lakes

People use lakes for a great variety of purposes. They have been catching lake fish for thousands of years. The New Testament of the Bible tells how Jesus and his followers went fishing on the Sea of Galilee (Lake Tiberias), between Israel and Syria. Most lakes are a source of fish, even the Caspian Sea. Salty though it is, the Caspian supports a great variety of fishes among them the sturgeon, which is the main source of the delicacy caviar. It also has a population of seals, which are hunted for their skins.

Lakes are of major importance for transportation. The Great Lakes make up North America's most important inland waterway system, and a large industrial area has grown up around their shores. All the world's major lakes have boats and ships on them – even Lake Titicaca, although it lies so high above sea level, has a steamship on it.

Lakes are ideal for windsurfing. This is a lake in East Germany.

Left Many people visit lakes just to appreciate their beauty. This is Buttermere in the Lake District of England.

Right Fish are an important resource of many lakes. Here are fishermen on Lake Victoria in Kenya.

Because lakes are a major source of water they are frequently used as reservoirs. In Britain, for example, many of the lakes in the Lake District supply water to cities in the north of England. Africa's largest lake, Lake Victoria, has been increased in depth by a little more than a yard by damming the Nile. This action has not only increased the area, it has added great quantities of water to the lake's capacity, so Lake Victoria is now both a reservoir and a lake.

The Dead Sea, which contains about 24 percent solid matter, is a rich source of minerals, and extraction plants on its shores produce bromine, gypsum, potash, and table salt.

Many lakes are used for sports and recreation. Some have sunny, sandy beaches. Sailing and water-skiing are popular lake sports, and Lake Windermere, in England, has been the scene of many world speedboat records.

Salt is often collected from salt lakes. This salt works is on the Dead Sea.

Artificial waterways

The advantages of rivers for transportation and irrigation were obvious from very early times. But rivers do not always go where they are wanted, and so people began to dig artificial waterways, or canals, in order to link rivers, lakes, or seas. Some of the earliest canals were made by people living in Babylonia about 3,000 years ago. Others were constructed by the Persians, the Greeks, and the Romans.

Canal building really got under way just before 1400 when the Dutch invented the lock, by which boats can pass from one level of water to another. The Dutch became great experts in canal construction, because the low level of their country made drainage canals essential.

Modern canal building began with the start of the Industrial Revolution in Britain in the 1700s. The first canals of this period were built to carry coal. The canal boom in Britain lasted until the development of railroads in the 1830s provided a better alternative for transporting goods and people.

Locks

A lock is a part of a canal or river that can be shut off by gates so that the water level can be raised or lowered and a boat can pass from one level of the river or canal to the next. Locks make it possible to build canals on land that isn't flat and to bypass rapids and waterfalls on rivers. A lock is operated by closing the bottom gate after the boat has entered the lock (1). A sluice gate (a small underwater door) in the top gate is opened and water flows into the lock, making the boat rise (2). When the water level in the lock is the same as that of the upper part of the canal, the top gate is opened and the boat passes through (3). The process is reversed if a boat is going downstream. The gates and sluices of most small locks are operated by hand, but on large modern locks electrical or hydraulic power is used. The gates are usually made of wood with iron or steel bands.

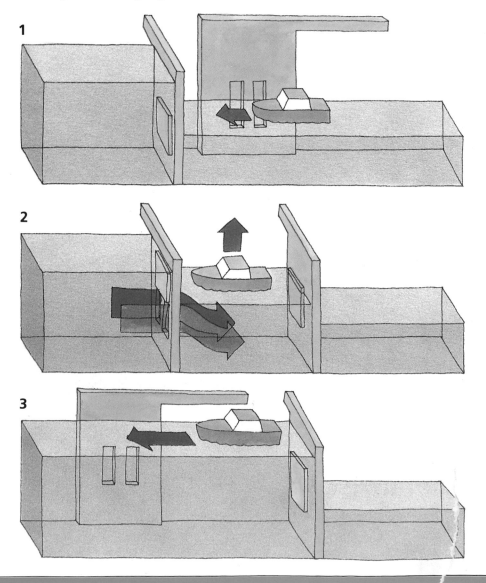

1

2

3

While British canals are largely disused, except for pleasure, those of continental Europe are very busy indeed. A canal network links the principal rivers of Belgium, France, Germany, and the Netherlands, and a canal linking the Rhine, the big river of the west, with the Danube, the major river of the east, was built in the 1960s. The Soviet Union also has a major canal network, linking the Baltic Sea with the Black Sea, and the Black Sea with the Caspian Sea, which uses existing rivers and lakes as well as canals.

Canals link many of the major rivers of the United States. The most important North American waterway is the St. Lawrence Seaway, which enables large ships to sail from the Atlantic Ocean to ports on the Great Lakes far inland. Two other important canals are both for ocean-going vessels: the Suez Canal, which passes through Egypt and links the Mediterranean Sea and the Red Sea, and the Panama Canal, which crosses Central America, linking the Atlantic and Pacific Oceans.

Above Left This is the Corinth Canal, a sea canal, that cuts across the Isthmus of Corinth in Greece.

Here where the great Mittelland Canal of Germany meets the Weser River a bridge has been constructed to carry the canal over the river.

Artificial lakes

The earliest known artificial lake was created in Egypt about 4,800 years ago. The remains of its dam, more than 340 ft (100 m) long, still exist. Other reservoirs were constructed in Mesopotamia (now part of Iraq) to hold water for irrigation. One was built at least 3,300 years ago. But it seems likely that beavers were building dams to create large ponds, in which they could construct their lodges, long before people tried to dam rivers.

In the Middle Ages, besides the millponds mentioned on page 22, people built hammer-ponds. Their purpose was to store water to drive the waterwheels that powered the mechanical hammers used in ironworking.

Today artificial lakes are made to store water for two main purposes: for drinking and to generate power. The world's biggest reservoir, in capacity, is the Bratsk, on the Angara River in the Soviet Union, completed in 1974. Almost as large is Lake Nasser, on the borders of Egypt and Sudan, in which the waters of the Nile are held back by the Aswan High Dam. The biggest artificial lake in surface area is Lake Volta, in Ghana.

These vast reservoirs are designed to provide hydroelectric power and water for irrigation. But a more common need is drinking water. Every large city needs one or more reservoirs, and the search is always on for more sites.

The dams needed for reservoirs are often very massive indeed. Some are built entirely of masonry or concrete, but frequently a huge bank of soil and rock is constructed, and faced with a casing of stone or concrete. A great deal of preliminary work is needed to divert the river across which the dam is to be built. For example, for the Itaipu Dam between Brazil and Paraguay, the Paraná River had to be diverted through a channel 1.2 miles (2km) long. The Itaipu Dam contains the world's largest, most productive hydroelectric plant.

Beavers probably created the first artificial lakes. They build dams of small logs, sticks, stones, and mud, which can last for many years. The dams slowly fill with silt, and a meadow is created, which can be used for grazing cattle.

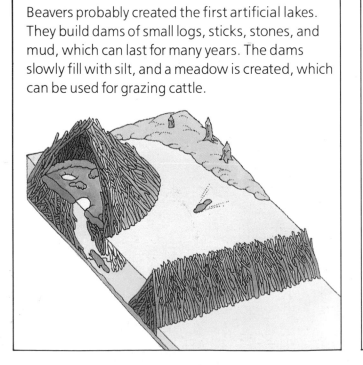

An important feature of artificial dams is the sluice gate. This allows excess water that could destroy the dam to be released in a controlled fashion. One simple form is a gate in the dam wall, which can be raised or lowered.

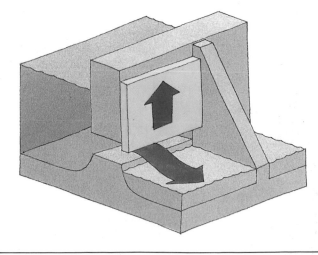

The Hoover Dam, a spectacular example of water engineering, has a number of uses. It provides protection from floods, water for irrigation and power generation, and an artificial lake for recreation.

Water pollution

People have been misusing rivers and lakes for thousands of years, by throwing or discharging into them quantities of unwanted matter. Some of this matter is relatively harmless, but much of it is very harmful indeed, not only to life in the water but to the people who live on its banks or – as is commonly the case along the major rivers of Asia – in houseboats moored by the banks or on boats such as barges that carry goods along rivers.

Water is polluted by three main things: sewage, industrial waste, and agricultural chemicals and waste. A river is an all-too-convenient means of disposing of sewage – it carries it away downstream to the sea. Until the development of modern methods of sewage treatment, human waste was discharged straight into the nearest river. Today, in developed countries, the sewage is treated to break down organic matter and remove harmful bacteria. Even so, harmful viruses and bacteria do get through, and people swimming in the river may then become seriously ill.

However, the effect of organic matter in a river is disastrous to the plants and animals in it. As bacteria and algae break down this waste matter, they use up a lot of the oxygen in the water, and there is not enough left for plants and animals.

Above In many countries, people treat waterways, such as this canal in London, as trash dumps, destroying much of their beauty.

Industrial pollution has developed since the start of the Industrial Revolution in the mid-1700s. Water is used for many industrial processes in enormous quantities. Industrial processes, from chemical production to the manufacturing of car tires, use millions of gallons of water every year, and although some of the water is cleaned and recycled, a great deal of it finds its way into rivers and lakes. Pollutants released into the air can also end up in rivers and lakes. Rain can dissolve chemicals in the smoke and gas released into the atmosphere and wash them into rivers and lakes. Acid rain is an example of this.

Left There are many possible sources of water pollution: **1** discharge of industrial waste, **2** leaking pipes, **3** run-off from crop spraying, **4** spillage of farm chemicals, **5** waste from farm animals, **6** inadequately treated sewage, **7** spillage from oil and chemical tankers, **8** leakage from car engines, **9** illegal dumping of industrial waste, **10** dumping of household waste, **11** ships and barges cleaning their tanks, **12** boats with leaky engines. One of the biggest possible sources of pollution is sewage, which must therefore be carefully treated.

Right One source of water pollution is the spraying of pesticides and herbicides. Rain washes them into rivers and lakes. This helicopter is spraying scrub in New Zealand.

Fighting water pollution

Since the end of World War II in 1945, governments everywhere have tried to tighten controls on the disposal of sewage and industrial waste. At the same time, a new peril has arrived, due to the modernization of farming and the wide-spread use of fertilizers and insecticides. These fertilizers and insecticides work very well on the fields to which they are applied. But they leave a residue that leaches into the soil, and ultimately finds its way into rivers and lakes.

DDT, an efficient insecticide, was developed during World War II, but by 1972 the United States government had to ban it because of the damage it was causing. Among the victims was the bald eagle, the national bird, which fed on fish and fish-eating birds that had absorbed great quantities of DDT in their food.

The Great Lakes of North America have been seriously affected by industrial and agricultural waste products. Three of the lakes – Michigan, Erie, and Ontario – are in particular severely affected by excess quantities of nitrogen and phosphorus. As a result they are threatened by a thick carpet of algae, which multiplies rapidly and uses up large quantities of oxygen as it dies and decomposes. Water can also be polluted by plants that are introduced into areas where they do not naturally occur. An example is the water hyacinth, a plant that spreads rapidly and has choked many waterways in Florida.

However, there have been several notable victories over water pollution. For example, the Thames, which flows through London, was originally a salmon river, but no salmon were seen after 1833, and in 1851 the smell from the river became so bad that sheets soaked in disinfectant were hung over the windows of the Houses of Parliament to try to keep out the stench. A clean-up of the river began in the 1950s, and by the 1980s salmon were once again seen in the Thames. The Willamette River in Oregon had, by the 1960s, become one of the dirtiest in the United States, polluted by sewage and the discharge from paper mills and food processing factories. It was unsafe for swimming and was shunned by trout, salmon, and other fish. A vigorous campaign produced a drop of 90 percent in waste discharge by 1972, and the fish returned to the river.

Cleaning-up the Thames
The Thames, the most famous of English rivers, was once known as a salmon river. As a result of river pollution, salmon had disappeared from the river by 1833. When a pleasure steamer, the *Princess Alice*, sank in the Thames in 1878 many of the 600 or so people who died were poisoned by the water rather than drowned. In recent years there has been a major effort to clean up the river. Its tributaries have been stocked with salmon and this one was caught in central London.